JOY

JOY

10 Minutes a Day to Color Your Way

CHER KAUFMANN

The Countryman Press
A division of W. W. Norton & Company
Independent Publishers Since 1923

Copyright 2016 © Cher Kaufmann

All rights reserved

Printed in Canada

For information about permission to reproduce
selections from this book, write to Permissions,
The Countryman Press, 500 Fifth
Avenue, New York, NY 10110

For information about special discounts
for bulk purchases, please contact
W. W. Norton Special Sales at
specialsales@wwnorton.com or 800-233-4830

The Countryman Press
www.countrymanpress.com

A division of W. W. Norton & Company, Inc.
500 Fifth Avenue, New York, NY 10110
www.wwnorton.com

978-1-58157-423-4 (pbk.)

10 9 8 7 6 5 4 3 2 1

To Lance, who always brightens
a room and makes people smile.

Introduction

Joy knows no beginning, middle, nor end. In Chinese medicine, joy is associated with expressions of the heart. Joy burns as bright as a flame, losing no brilliance as it inspires: Think of it as a candle lighting another candle. Joy is light. Sometimes the light is soft and low like a pilot light, but ever steady and ready to flare up at a moment's notice. Joy can provide warmth the same way a bonfire does. Joy is easily shared and has long-lasting benefits to emotional health as well as mental and physical wellbeing. The human brain has the ability to reset according to continually processed thoughts. What this means is the very idea of holding joyful thoughts on a consistent basis will literally begin to eradicate the space held for thoughts less than joyful.

Maintaining joyful thoughts for extended periods of time and making it a habit to think with joy has the potential to change the brain and the person. Brain-body connection researchers such as Dr. Andrew Newberg and Mark Robert Waldman discovered contemplative thought in the form of meditation reinforces neural processing of the brain. Visualizing with a strong emotion of joy, gratitude, or love can aid in lowering anxiety and depression by redirecting synapses to more joyfully directed pathways. Dr. Joe Dispenza, lecturer and researcher in neural processing, opines that in an average day, we repeat up to 90 percent of our thoughts from the previous day. He suggests further that we have more control over repeated thoughts once we become aware of them. What if you slowly changed your routine thoughts to ones of magnificence?

Imagine spending 10 minutes a day, with attentive focus on joy and happiness. Little by little, a joyful outlook can be yours.

"The present moment is filled with joy and happiness," says Zen Master Thích Nhat Hanh. "If you are attentive, you will see it."

How to Use This Book

- Start your day at any time—morning, afternoon, or night—with reflections in these pages.
- You may find the book helpful to read at your leisure in small, 10-minute blocks. You may reflect and contemplate the important messages any time during your day.
- You can find calm by coloring the pages provided that are paired with passages and inspirational quotes. Use this activity as a relaxing coloring meditation.
- There are a dozen lined pages with "joy prompts" for jotting down special memories and ideas.
- Blank pages also contain simple drawing prompts for your moments of artistic creativity.
- Randomly open to a page to see what inspiration you might gain on a given day.

*"You are the sky. Everything else—
it's just the weather."*

—Pema Chödrön

List three small things you can
do today to bring you more joy.

10-Minute Meditation

Joy Glow

Sit in a comfortable position—wherever you are is fine. Close your eyes. Relax your hands, cupped open as if holding a ball. Imagine this ball is made of light, glowing brightly, warmly, and comfortably. Every time you breathe outward, allow your hands to gently move outward, letting the ball slowly get bigger and bigger.

Imagine all the moments of happiness are bouncing around in this golden ball. Can you feel the light and warmth of the ball change when joy, happiness, and bliss begin to add to the radiance? Bring the ball into your heart; imagine it filling you with a radiant glow.

Breathe naturally, smile softly.

"I've got nothing to do today but smile."

—Paul Simon

Today I am joyful
in ways that are light
and playful.

Joy has an effervescence that bubbles up,
lights up a room, and delights the air with giggles.
If joy was a flower, what would it look like?

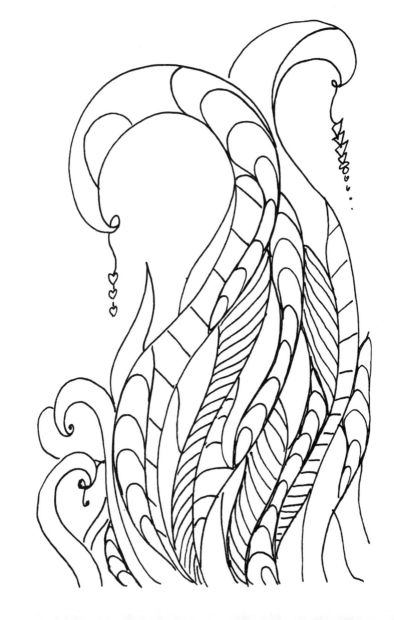

Everyone's heard of the butterfly effect.
Now think about the giggle effect.
Have you ever started one?

LAUGHTER

Years ago, I attended a workshop with 600 attendees. On the far right side of the room, in the front row, someone had the giggles. Close by, others began to chuckle quietly. Soon, like a wave on the beach, snickers washed through the room. Like waves, the sound ebbed and flowed as people caught their breath and then started anew. One woman stood up from the front row of my area and ran to the door to leave the room. She almost made it before she burst out into uncontrollable laughter and spilled her joyous sounds with the same grace as throwing a bucket of water on the crowd.

The laughter was infectious. Hundreds of people were giggling for no reason. That irresistible, spontaneous laughter continued for hours. When was the last time you laughed with unrelenting bliss?

LAUGHTER CHALLENGE

·MY·
Laugh Out Loud
😄 MOMENTS

1.

2.

3.

"Time you enjoy wasting is not wasted time."

—Marthe Troly-Curtin

10-Minute Meditation

Sun Breathing

Sit in a comfortable position in the sun or in partial sun, cross-legged on the floor or upright in a chair with your feet flat touching the earth. Sit up straight and tall. Relax your hands. Take a deep breath, allowing your shoulders to rise slightly and naturally on the inhale; then soften your shoulders, let them drop down, and roll your shoulder blades closer together on the exhale. This creates a natural expansion to open the area of the heart. In this quietness, just breathe.

Feel the warmth of the sun where it touches your skin. Is the sun warming your clothing?

10-Minute Meditation
(continued)

Imagine the rays of the sun as a warm, loving embrace. Can you feel your skin absorb the heat? Can you feel the heat move into your body, receiving this joyful gift from the sun?

On your next inhale, breathe in the sun. Breathe in the warmth of the light. Maybe you felt your head turn upward slightly; maybe your cheeks smiled in the dance of warmth. The sun gives blissful energy to every person, plant, rock, and creature on Earth. The cosmic glow lights up your cells, feeds them, and assists in growth. Feel the soft pulse, a gentle rush that moves between your body and the sun. This rhythm of sun and body is joy swirling and dancing in you. Breathe in the sun, breathe in joy, breathe out pleasure, and breathe out enjoyment. Be joy today. Be the sun.

Today I am aware
that my footprints
matter. Where I go,
what I do, who
I am, matters.

Instead of your usual footprints in the sand,
if you could leave a trail of joy, what would it look like?
Doodle your best "joy prints" on the page.

Describe yourself including the word "joyfully"
before every verb. What do you like to do for fun?
What are you good at? What is the first and
last thing you do every day?

THE SUN ALWAYS SHINES

Years ago, waiting in a plane for takeoff, I looked out my window. It was winter and cold; light rain and snow were falling. Bundled-up workers scurried to move luggage. I was glad to be inside. The plane took off and we emerged from the clouds, rising above the haze. There, greeting us like a smile from a friend, the sun illuminated the sky— soft pinks and golden yellows dusted the tops of the puffs. The striking difference left me momentarily stunned.

Oh, glorious realization—the sun is always shining! Even if we don't see it, even if nature has to bring rain and clouds, the sun, with luminescent wisdom, is waiting for us. On days when you are feeling in the shadows, remember the sun is always shining, waiting patiently for the clouds to move on, gently warming and coloring the surfaces. There is great love and joy in the gem of the sun.

"Let us be grateful to the people who make us happy; they are the charming gardeners who make our souls blossom."

—Marcel Proust

Draw your version of a rainbow (it does not have
to look like the one you drew as a child!) Be creative.

10-Minute Meditation

Breeze Release

Imagine your hand waving in the wind out the window. Ride the highs and lows of the breeze in aerodynamic rhythm, caressed by the airflow from fingertip to palm to wrist and over your arm. So gentle the pleasure of the breeze, feeling the softness of wind blowing away any extra thoughts or cares.

Feel the peacefulness and gladness swirl in this slow-motion moment. Feel your heart lighten, brighten, and fill with wonder and possibility. What if you let go with your whole body, releasing all unnecessary stress from your body and mind into the wind? You now have more room in your heart space. Joyfulness.

Soft, unhurried happiness expands and begins to play with the wind as well. Sometimes, the breeze will remind you—with a gentle twirling of your hair or a tug on your shirt—to let go the unnecessary thoughts and make room for more delight. And so you do: breathe out and blow over your palm, send out the excess as simply as a dandelion releasing her seeds.

"Happiness is when what you think, what you say, and what you do are in harmony."

—Mahatma Gandhi

Joy

Today I am listening to music that brings me joy and makes me dance, smile, and sing.

Finish the sentence with a ridiculous amount
of happy, joyful, smiley words.
My heart smiles when . . .

"After silence, that which comes nearest to expressing the inexpressible is music."

—Aldous Huxley

MUSIC

Music is a universal language. Sounds vibrate in the air through the trees, in the songs of birds, and in our voices. Using music to build happiness is easier than people realize. Lyrics, beat, rhythm, and, in some cases, the vocal quality all move through the body, mind, and spirit, luring the musical experience to be intertwined and entertained. Music can mark a happy time in our lives and it can express that which we are unable to say with words to each other and to ourselves. Music can fill your heart, lighten the mood, and replenish the smooth and effortlessness of being. Turn on your favorite song and turn up the volume!

> *"Sometimes your joy is the source of your smile, but sometimes your smile can be the source of your joy."*

—Thich Nhat Hanh

10-Minute Meditation

Tap It In

To save an especially lovely feeling of happiness, friendship, joy, and awakened sunshiny vitality, tap it in. Literally. Allow full focus to be on the feeling of happiness.

Gently, with a soft touch, tap the sternum in the center of your chest with your fingertips. Tap with the intention of having your body and mind remember this feeling.

With the easy tapping, imagine the feeling being sent deep inside to all your cells, and residing in your happy heart. Then, whenever you need to remember that feeling, you can always revisit it by tapping your heart (the sternum, where you tapped before). This will reawaken your happiness. With attentive focus and a smile, see the delight inside with gratitude. With practice, you will eventually get to a place where you no longer need to tap anything to bring the cheerfulness forward—it will be instantaneously available.

Write a quick list of ordinary items that make you happy (an authentic giggle, hot tea on a cold day, seeing a dog on a walk), just whatever comes to the top of your thoughts. Feel free to add to it anytime.

Today I am a joy
finder, finding joy
in people, places,
and things.

*"You will never be happy if you
continue to search for what happiness
consists of. You will never live if you
are looking for the meaning of life."*

—Albert Camus

Fill this page with stars.

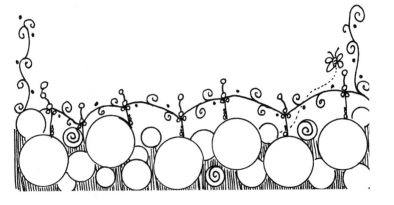

Somewhere, Something **Incredible** is waiting to be **Known.**

—Carl Sagan

"When you do things from your soul, you feel a river moving in you, a joy."

—Rumi

There's a hidden heart in the next drawing.
Does your heart have a hidden "happy"
waiting to be discovered?

10-Minute Meditation

Walking Meditation

If you are lucky enough to have access to a labyrinth, nature path, or hiking trail, consider making your trek a walking meditation of joy. If you have access to a sidewalk, you can do this as well. For the sidewalk, imagine every time you step over a crack or division in the cement, you increase the joy felt for a particular person, place, or thing, completely supported by the enormous presence of the earth below you. Imagine the cracks in the sidewalk as a means for the earth to reach you in a sneaky way that no one else can see.

For the nature walkers, imagine every tree you pass and every rounded curve as an amplifier of your thoughts. Imagine the trees expanding your happiness level upward and outward. This simple act of meditation will halt arguments in your head, complaints and misgivings of the heart, and it will make room for thoughts of connectivity, love, happiness, and peacefulness. This can literally change your day. Feel the power of your thoughts by simply being aware of them with every crack you step over, or every tree you pass.

"Mighty oaks from little acorns grow."
Joy can work the same way. Have you ever done
something reluctantly that has brought you great joy?

....

...✳...

....

....♡......

....

..............@...

....

....

....⚘.............

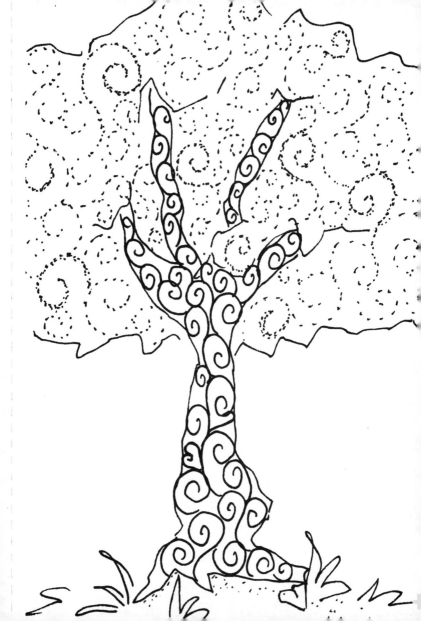

"Follow your bliss and the universe will open doors where there were only walls."

—Joseph Campbell

Create your Own Designs

ADD ON • EMBELLISH

DANCE

Dance is being with the music—not simply listening. Feeling the drumbeat, bouncing, rocking, and tapping your foot in a class or in your living room—it makes you happy. Fast-moving salsa, hip-hop, party dancing, the precision of waltz, or the grace of ballet invites every system in the body to communicate together. Even watching another person dance can create a stir inside you, mirroring the energy so you feel energetically lifted by the movement. Pick out one really great song you love and dance to it!

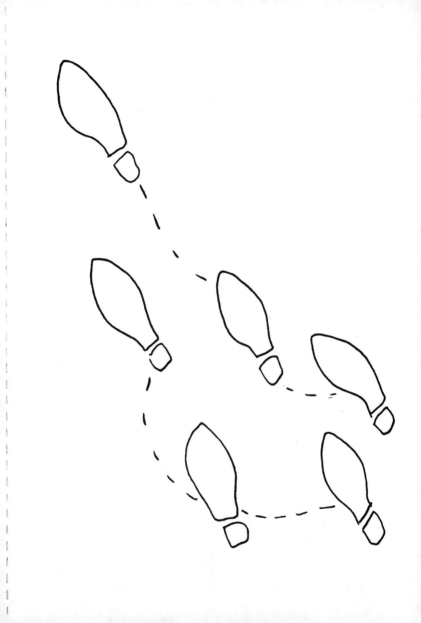

Pick a happy shape (like a flower, spiral or
balloons) and fill the page with as many as you can.
You can color them if that makes you happy!

98 Mpe